How Does Your Choir Grow?

D1403288

How Does
Your Choir Grow?

David F. Donathan

LINCOLN CHRISTIAN COLLEGE AND SEMINARY

Abingdon Press
Nashville

HOW DOES YOUR CHOIR GROW?

Copyright © 1995 by Abingdon Press

All rights reserved.
No part of this work may be reproduced or transmitted in any form or by any means, electronic or mechanical, including photocopying and recording, or by any information storage or retrieval system, except as may be expressly permitted by the 1976 Copyright Act or in writing from the publisher. Requests for permission should be addressed to Abingdon Press, P.O. Box 801, 201 Eighth Avenue South, Nashville TN 37202.

This book is printed on recycled, acid-free paper.

Library of Congress Cataloging-in-Publication Data

Donathan, David F.
    How does your choir grow? / David F. Donathan.
      p.   cm.
    ISBN 0-687-01075-6 (acid-free paper)
    1. Choirs (Music)   2. Choral conducting.   3. Church music—Instruction
  and study.
MT88.D66   1995
782.5'171—dc20
                                            94-44770
                                                CIP
                                               MN

95 96 97 98 99 00 01 02 03 04—10 9 8 7 6 5 4 3 2 1

MANUFACTURED IN THE UNITED STATES OF AMERICA

This book is fondly dedicated to

The Chancel Choir
Christ Church United Methodist
Charleston, West Virginia

and

The Chancel Choir
First United Methodist Church
Dalton, Georgia

Two choirs with which I have had the privilege to
work and whose willingness to grow
led to the development
and refining of the program described
in this book.

594

90728

Contents

Introduction

One of the most frustrating things church choir directors are facing today is recruiting new choir members. Whether recruiting children, youth, or adults as new members, this process can be time-consuming and often leads to frustration and doubt. In most cases, growth will not occur in a church music program without the assistance of a well-thought-out plan. There are endless factors that can determine the growth of a church music program, such as, the relationship among the church's staff members, the relationship among the choir members, the perception of the church's music program in the community, and even the church's music facilities. This book is designed to help you come up with a common-sense, concrete method for developing a long-term growth plan for a volunteer church choir. While this program development is going on, you can also prepare for this expected growth by analyzing the physical needs of an expanded program, including implementation of activities to promote ownership, fellowship, and a sense of worth.

The small support groups of the sixties and seventies are resurfacing in the nineties. People need a place where they feel a sense of belonging and fellowship; a place where they can forget their troubles and be uplifted; a place where they can share and feel unconditional love and at the same time contribute to the life of the church and the spread of the gospel. A church choir, when developed like a small group, can be one of the most rewarding small groups in the church.

The cartoons in this book were drawn by a talented youth by the name of Aaron Crothers, a member of Christ Church United Methodist, the church I presently serve. I am very grateful for his willingness to create these humorous drawings for this book.

David F. Donathan

Chapter One

Analyzing Your Present Situation

"You don't need me to sing in the choir!"
"You don't need me. You already have plenty of women in the choir."
"You don't need me because you have plenty of men in the choir."
"I can't sing."
"The choir is too good. I would only mess things up."
"I don't have the time."

Every choir director, at one time or another, has heard these excuses. With these excuses constantly impeding growth, how can volunteer church choirs grow and develop? How can choir directors keep their enthusiasm when the answer to pleas for new members is always no?

These excuses are based mostly on preconceived notions. The way to get beyond them is through a concentrated program of education and recruitment. In order to develop a program to fit the needs of a particular church music ministry, first study your music program as it currently operates.

The first and most important step is to be in a spirit of prayer. It is virtually impossible to proceed in this endeavor without asking for God's guidance, because anything that is done in the church should be done to glorify God and carry out God's will and desire for the church. Next, sit down with your senior pastor and share with him or her the dreams for the music ministry. It is important that the senior pastor be supportive in what you are trying to do; otherwise, the growth efforts may suffer. Once the senior pastor endorses your efforts, share it with other key people in the church leadership family to whom you are responsible. Once the key people are supporting your efforts, it's time to get busy.

It is important for directors to know their group inside and out. Discovering this information will help determine a plan for growth. It is amazing to discover the number of choir directors who do not know their choir members. Many don't even know first names. To begin developing a long-range growth plan, first, analyze the music ministry as it is now. It is vital that honesty be foremost in the analysis for your efforts to be fruitful. If the church utilizes a computer program like the UMIS System (United Methodist Information Services), gathering material will be relatively easy. Otherwise, you will need to do some legwork looking through church records.

Here is a series of questions that need to be addressed:

Choir Survey

1. What is the average age of the choir? What vocal sections need building?

Determining this will help you come up with a possible target group from which to recruit.

2. What are the work schedules of the choir members?

Are the choristers office workers, construction workers, retired? Would their jobs normally interfere with the chosen rehearsal time? Recent job cutbacks have resulted in fewer people doing more work for the same pay by working longer hours. Studying the professions of your choir members will aid you in understanding the demands on their time. Understanding these demands will also assist you when planning special rehearsals and program events.

3. Does the choir want to grow, knowing that this growth brings in new members?

Some choirs don't want to grow. They feel things are fine the way they are. Why bring in newcomers? You need to find out what the consensus is in your choir. On the average, most volunteer choirs are willing to grow.

4. What kind of personalities are in the choir?

Do the choir members get along with one another? Is the group friendly to newcomers? Always be careful with this. It's not uncommon for people to quit singing in the choir because "that person" joined! Try to figure out if the choir is made up of cliques that will be hard for new members to enter. Many times, personal conflicts among choir members can be traced back, unfortunately, to the choir director.

5. Is the rehearsal time convenient for the majority of the members?

"We've been rehearsing on Thursday evening ever since this church was built! We can't change the rehearsal time." Does that statement sound like a "churchism" or what! The truth is, you may be missing out on a large number of participants because your rehearsal time is inconvenient. In today's world where time is quickly becoming a precious commodity, determine the most effective time for rehearsals. The best way to approach this is to have an open discussion during a rehearsal and let the choir share in the decision-making process. The issue of time is an even bigger problem for churches with two or more adult choirs singing for two or more different services.

Answers to questions 3 and 5 must include input from the current choir members. Any decisions made in these areas without the choir's involvement could lead to alienation between the director and the choir.

6. Does child care need to be provided during rehearsal?

The answer to this is a resounding *yes,* especially if one of the target groups is young adults who would probably have school-aged children. If you don't offer child care, start now. If you already have child care, why not take it a step further and make it a structured time. You could go beyond child care by creating a special "small group" format for the children of choir members. Personally, I have two children who come to the church during choir because my wife also sings in the choir. Our two daughters like being there because they have such a wonderful time in child care. The key is to get a winsome and capable person or persons to take charge of the choir child care program.

Here are a few personal questions for the director to answer:

Director's Survey

1. Are my rehearsals fun and uplifting with time for spiritual growth, or are they always serious, laborious, or without focus?

An entirely separate book could be written on ways for directors to improve their rehearsal techniques and interpersonal skills. Be honest with yourself in order to improve in these areas. Answer this question, "If I were in my choir, would I keep coming week after week?"

Another issue to keep in mind is the length of rehearsal. Most volunteer choir rehearsals should be no more than one and a half hours, especially if your rehearsal is on a weeknight. After an hour and a half, any rehearsal becomes laborious. In The United Methodist Church, members are asked to serve by committing time, talents, gifts, and service. Today, time is a precious commodity. If rehearsal starts at 7:30 P.M., start at 7:30 P.M., not 7:40. Be sure to end on time. Always going overtime will only frustrate the choristers. Be a good steward of your choir members' time commitments for rehearsal, once the best time for rehearsal is determined. Well-planned rehearsals also give the director peace of mind. Don't forget the reason for rehearsing: to glorify God through music!

2. What kinds and styles of music does the choir usually prepare for worship?

Here is another loaded question and the basis for yet another book. Nevertheless, it needs to be addressed. The answer is partially determined by the church's tradition and style of worship. At the same time, there is a need to be open-minded about new music. When planning music, remember that there are people in the congregation who appreciate all types of music, including jazz, contemporary Christian, classical, and top forty. A good music director will search diligently for well-written anthems inclusive of all styles of composition. Never stop searching for new music. Musical offerings should meet two basic criteria:

1. It must be well written.
2. The text must be based on sound theological principles.

Always look for texts that praise God, not humanity. Never pick a piece simply because you like it. Music in a worship service should serve a functional purpose: to enable the congregation to experience the presence of God. It should lift up the listener to new heights of awareness. This is why selecting appropriate music is so important. If music is planned simply as a performance piece for the choir, the choir and their director have both failed in their role as worship leaders and therefore alienate themselves from the ministry of music. Church musicians must be dedicated to excellence in music for the church, and if the end result sounds professional, that's fine. Just keep in mind the primary reason for planning the music.

Now that all of the information has been gathered, it needs to be stored and processed. Processing the data should provide a basic profile of the group and help determine a course of action. It would also be a good idea to have a smaller group chosen from the choir to help gather and process the information and help develop the growth plan. Remember, including the choir in the decision-making process will give them ownership in developing a direction for the future.

Stacking the Deck in Your Favor

Let's face it, churches are highly political. Sometimes, politics can stand in the way of growth and development. In order to assist in planning for the growth of the program, see that certain music ministry participants are placed on all of the significant committees of the church. In most cases, the music staff person can be included on the committee that nominates people for trustees, the committee on finance, and the general governing committees. Nominating music ministry participants for these committees gives the ministry a voice on every governing body of the church. If money is needed for renovations, the person representing the music ministry on the board of trustees can speak for the director and help influence the decisions. This kind of participation gives the music program a voice in the decision making for the church, an important element in growth and development.

Chapter Two

Developing a Long–Range Growth Plan

Determining Your Strategy

After gathering the data, the next thing to be done is compiling all of the information collected, and, from this compilation, developing a long-range plan that suits the growth of the church and the music ministry. First, take the questions and their answers and simply list the information on a sheet of paper. This profile of the group will highlight strengths, weaknesses, and areas that need attention. With this information you can also determine the median age of the choir, which is important if the long-range plan leads toward involving more people from a certain age bracket.

Let's take a hypothetical situation in order to illustrate how to analyze the material gathered. Let's say that you are in a new position as a choir director or director of music ministries. You are coming into this new job knowing a little about the music ministry, but there is a need to know more. You sit down and complete all of the questions in the previous chapter with the help of the church secretary and members of the choir. After listing all of the information on a sheet of paper, you determine that the average age of your choir is fifty; many members are retired; they've known one another for years; and, they are set in the way they do things as a group.

Every director needs to know their choir members on a personal basis. The director sometimes takes on a clergy model, being there for support, personal discussions, and leadership. There is no excuse for not knowing your people. You may have worked with them compiling information, but do you really know them? If you are new in the position, the last thing you want to do is come in and upset everything by doing what *you* think is best for the group. First, get to know the choir and see where they stand on certain issues like growth and new members. This is the time to plant ideas as "seeds" that will grow and develop over time. After developing this relationship with the choir, then slowly share with them your desire to increase involvement in the program. Help them see the possibilities that lie in the growth of the church's music ministry.

Setting a Goal

Now that you have all of the information, have analyzed it and, if necessary, determined a target group, setting a numerical goal is the next step. In order to set a goal, physical constraints may have to be kept in mind. You should plan on a 60 to 70 percent attendance ratio on any given Sunday. In order to establish a more accurate percentage, count the choir members present each Sunday for at least a month and then determine the average attendance percentage. Since the time before the service is usually hectic, why not count the choir members during the sermon and figure out the percentage in attendance before the closing hymn!

For example, if there are twenty people in the choir, and fourteen show up on a regular basis each Sunday, this is 70 percent singing on Sunday mornings. In order to determine a numerical goal for the recruiting campaign, take the maximum seating in the choir loft and add 30 percent. This new number can then serve as a membership goal. If your choir loft seats thirty, add 30 to 40 percent to arrive at about forty. Forty then becomes your membership goal. When allowing for a 60 to 70 percent ratio on any given Sunday, this leaves twenty-five to thirty choir members each Sunday, or in this case a full choir loft. This also means that a choir of twenty would need to double its membership. While that may sound impossible, keep in mind, "With God, all things are possible." With the help of the scheduled publicity to be discussed later, setting a high goal will also help eliminate preconceived notions, such as, "You don't need any more women (or men) in the choir."

Also keep in mind the number of people that can sit comfortably in the rehearsal space. A larger membership may mean that the rehearsal needs to be moved to a larger room or that enlargement of the choir area may be necessary (to be discussed in chapter 4). I recommend *not* rehearsing in the choir loft. Many times, the worship space is a more live, reverberant space, which is great for musical offerings in a service, but in my opinion, is bad for rehearsal purposes. A drier acoustic in which to rehearse will enable the director to hear more of the things that may need to be fixed before the anthem is offered on Sunday morning. If you need adults for two choirs, be sure to keep your goals for each group separate, and be specific as to when you need people to sing.

Timetable

It is important to remember that this entire program will be a long-term project possibly taking up to a year or more when counting time for analysis, planning, getting to know people, training people, self-improvement, implementation of the new member campaign, and wrap-up. A good time to do the study of the choir and its membership is during the summer when things move at a much slower pace in church music. This is also a good time for the director of the choir to seek out self-improvement workshops and conferences. The best time to implement a long-range plan is anytime. The best time to implement a new member recruiting campaign as part of the long-range plan is in the late summer, about three weeks before the school term starts and rehearsals for the fall resume. This plan gives everybody a fresh start with a new season. Another possible time for a new member campaign is at the beginning of the calendar year. Each director must consider the church's schedule and plan on doing this new member campaign when it would yield the best results. Chapter 3 describes the implementation of a new member campaign, which is probably the most important step in the entire long-range plan.

Disseminating the Information

Now that all of the background work has been done, it is time to present the goals you and your committee have been formulating. It is important to get the present choir members excited about the new member campaign because they will have a direct part in the implementation of the program. Share the goals and dreams with as many groups in the church as possible. The more people who hear first-hand the goals and dreams, the more response you may have. Attend the meetings of the worship committee, trustees, program council, and administrative board, to name a few.

Publicize your intentions and goals throughout the church, including church school classes. Be sure to use the church newsletter. Keep the campaign fun and uplifting. The main thing is to get the word out that the choir wants to grow. Be sure to use your numerical goal in the information.

*I know he wants new choir members, but
this is ridiculous!*

Chapter Three

Developing a New Member Packet

As mentioned in the previous chapter, one very important element of the long-range plan is the new member campaign. This campaign is a plan to contact people who might be interested in participating in the music ministry. Preparing the campaign packet will once again involve the current members of the choir. When completed, the packet will include everything the choir members need to help increase involvement in the music ministry.

Obtaining a List of Potential New Members

The best place to obtain the first set of potential new members is from the list of new church members. Often, these new members are looking for a place to get involved. Statistics show that if new members are not assimilated into the life of the church within the first few weeks, they will end up becoming inactive and eventually drop off of the church roster.

The main list of potential choristers will come from the current choir members. Keep in mind that these potential members do not have to be church members. This new member campaign is a wonderful tool to reach the unchurched. Since the choir members are providing the list, chances are this list of prospective members will contain names of friends or work acquaintances of the choir members. Growth experts today say that people will attend church when invited by a friend. One night at rehearsal, have the choir write down names of people they perceive as being potential choir members. It is important that the names be written down because you will need to refer to these names later in developing the packet. If the choir traditionally breaks for the summer, be sure to obtain a list of names before stopping in May or June.

Include in your list names from church school classes that are in your target group, or that are known to sing during Sunday classes. Another source is the list of visitors that have been attending regularly. Maybe the reason they keep returning is for the music. Check with the person who is in charge of visitor statistics, such as the membership secretary or evangelism committee chairperson, for additional leads.

Also, as the director, look over lists of former choir members and find out what has happened to those who are not attending anymore.

Be sure to keep an accurate list of names, complete with phone numbers. This list will be the key to the entire new member campaign.

For ease of reference and planning, be sure to list the names numerically as follows:

Potential New Member List

1. Name   Phone Number
2. Name   Phone Number
3. Name   Phone Number

It is not uncommon to have up to fifty names. The more names on the list, the higher the success rate will be.

Organizing Your Current Members

When laying out your timetable for the new member campaign, include three weeks for calling and contacting potential new members. This calling campaign is the heart of the entire growth process and will, once again, involve the current members of the choir. If this new member campaign is to succeed, choir members must have an active role in the process. Involving them directly will create a sense of ownership in the project and add to the overall success of the plan.

To involve choir members, organize a telephone campaign in which each current member calls potential new members. Here's how to set up the telephone campaign.

At the top of a sheet of paper type the phrase, "WEEK OF _____." Type the names of current choir members alphabetically down the left side of the paper. Place a short, blank line after each name. After doing this, make three copies of the list and lay them out on a table.

If this campaign is to take place in the late summer, first, set the date for your first rehearsal in the fall. From this date, back up three or four full weeks. This date then becomes the first week of the calling campaign. On the top of the first sheet where it says, "WEEK OF _____," place the corresponding date for the first week of the campaign using Monday's date. On the other two sheets, place the Monday dates for the next two weeks. The task is to assign the current choir members to call the people on the potential new members list. When assigning callers to potential new members, keep in mind things that people might have in common, such as, their age, the area of town where they live, activities in the church, and even church school classes. This way, these people already have something in common. Go down the potential members list and assign each one to a choir member for the first week. For week two, reassign the potential member to a different member of the choir than the one who called during week one. For the third week, reassign that person one more time to yet a different choir member. This way, the potential member receives three calls from three different people offering three completely different opinions and outlooks on the choir program. Statistics show that people need to hear things more than once before they actually sink in.

Calling Schedule

WEEK OF August 3

Choir Member's Name	Calling Potential Member
John Doe	#1
Ruth Smith	#4
Jim King	#10

Calling Schedule

WEEK OF August 10

Choir Member's Name	Calling Potential Member
John Doe	#2
Ruth Smith	#27
Jim King	#4

Every once in a while, a person states that he or she does not want to be bothered with any further phone calls. In this case, the caller is instructed to notify the other members of the choir who have been assigned to call this person and tell them not to call. There is no reason for badgering someone into joining. On the other hand, during the campaign, other names will surface. If this happens, let the choir members take the initiative to have two other people make a contact.

Overall Instructions

It is necessary to provide a list of instructions for all people involved in the phone campaign. A sample list of instructions is shown below. You will need to adapt these instructions to your own situation, adding and deleting items where necessary. Things that could be mentioned in addition to the items listed in number 2 of the calling instructions are: the dates of the fall choir retreat, any trips that might be planned for the year, even whether new robes are to be ordered. This instruction sheet should be included in the complete packet when assembled later, so be as concise as possible.

Assembling the Packet

Enlist the help of your planning committee and assemble the total packet in the following order:

1. Colorful and humorous front cover
2. Letter of support from the director
3. Instructions page
4. Potential New Members List
5. Calling Schedule—Week One
6. Calling Schedule—Week Two
7. Calling Schedule—Week Three
8. One or two blank pages for notes
9. Back cover

Try to make the packet look professional. Take time and care in laying out the pages and the cover. Demand good quality from your printing machine (if possible!) and staple the entire packet down the left-hand side to create a booklet. Mail the packet about five to seven days before the first week of the phone campaign to everyone participating.

Campaign Follow-up

Each week during the calling campaign, mail a reminder card to the choir members reminding them to make their appointed calls. Don't let them slack in their willingness to be involved. This phone campaign is extremely important to the future growth of the choir. There is nothing wrong with reminding them on a weekly basis. During the second week of the campaign, use your choir committee to call the choir members to check on the progress of the campaign. This will help in finding weak spots, if any, in the campaign.

It is also a good idea for the director to call people who are seriously considering joining the choir. This shows potential new members that the director cares about the group and is genuinely interested in their involvement. When the campaign is completed, bring your committee back together and analyze the success of the campaign. When the campaign is over, you should have an idea of what to expect for your first rehearsal.

New Member Campaign
Calling Instructions

Please read over the information carefully before making your assigned phone calls. Find your name on the calling schedule each week. Beside your name is the number of the potential choir member you are to call that week. Refer back to the Potential Members List to obtain the person's phone number.

1. Plan on making your phone calls in the evening. If talking to a person you do not know, introduce yourself as a member of the Chancel Choir and explain that you would like to talk for a few minutes.

2. Be sure to discuss the following items:

    a. Ask the person's opinion of the present program being offered.

    b. What kinds of music does he or she like to hear in a church service?

    c. Is any other family member involved in the program?

    d. Share your own personal experience of singing in the choir.

    e. Be sure to mention that a nursery for rehearsal is provided.

3. End the conversation in a polite manner thanking the person for his or her time. Encourage the person to consider joining the choir. Also be sure to mention that there will be a new members reception before the first rehearsal.

4. This is not a conclusive list. Feel free to add names to the list if any come up during the campaign. Be sure to assign other people to call if appropriate.

5. During the third week, remind people of the upcoming rehearsal. If you like, offer to pick them up and bring them with you.

6. There are several blank pages at the end of this booklet

for your own notes. Keep a record of responses to your questions.

7. If anyone is adamant about NOT receiving any other calls, refer back to the list of assigned calls and contact that choir member telling them not to call this person.

GOOD LUCK AND HAPPY PHONING!

Chapter Four

Analysis of the Physical Needs of a Music Ministry

I n planning for long-range growth in a music ministry, the physical needs of an expanded music ministry must also be addressed. Proper space in the rehearsal and worship areas will greatly determine the effect an expanded ministry will have. A study of the rehearsal area should be done at the same time the group's analysis is being done. Let the assigned committee help with this study. In his book *Building an Effective Music Ministry,* William J. Reynolds goes to great detail on how to prepare for the physical needs of a music ministry. Listed below are key elements Reynolds refers to that need to be addressed for the adult space requirements:

1. The capacity of the choir loft should be at least 10 percent of the permanent seating in the sanctuary.

When analyzing the worship space, determine the 10 percent ratio, then round up to the nearest 5. If the sanctuary seats 315 people, 10 percent will equal 31.5 seats in the choir loft, or 35 seats when rounded up. This may have a direct impact on your numerical goal for involvement.

2. Does the choir room have a flexible layout?

A rehearsal space must be flexible, especially if it is used for more than adult rehearsals. Many people prefer rehearsing on risers for sight and sound purposes. But using risers in the rehearsal space limits the functionality of the room. Some churches use a regular classroom during the week for rehearsal purposes because of space limitations. Whatever the case, a flexible room layout will let you change the room as the program demands. When the room is flexible in seating arrangements, rehearse in one configuration, and on Sunday morning, rearrange the chairs so they are set up as they are in the choir loft. A flexible room layout will also be helpful if the room is utilized by the multiple choirs from varying age groups.

3. Does the rehearsal space allow fifteen square feet per member of the choir?

Space is important, and lack of space will create a cramped feeling during rehearsal. A new choir member could end up thinking, "There is no room for me," and not come back. A choir with twenty members needs 300 square feet of floor space; a choir of thirty members needs 450 square feet of floor space, and so on. Children need twenty-five square feet per person.

4. Is there a decent rehearsal instrument in the rehearsal space?

This is definitely a necessity. How can the choir sing in tune if the piano is out of tune or if it doesn't function well? Many choirs today are turning to high-quality, full-size, electronic pianos.

5. Do the chairs encourage good posture?

Be sure your chairs encourage good posture. As the director, your insistence on good posture will help.

6. Is there adequate storage for equipment?

Be sure to allow space to store instruments and equipment that are owned by the church. Leaving instruments in the rehearsal space will clutter the space, making it seem smaller. It will also be subject to more abuse, especially from the child that is always drumming on something.

7. Are there convenient robing areas?

This may be considered a luxury; however, separate robing facilities are recommended for men and women if at all possible. Many times in the summer, women may prefer to remove some of their clothing before putting on a choir robe for a service in order to stay cool.

8. Does the space have a good traffic pattern?

Can people get into the choir room without tripping over the handbells, extra chairs, and such? Be sure people can move within the space.

9. Does it have good lighting?

You may not have much control over lighting if you are assigned to using a regular classroom. Improper lighting will make the room too dark. This will have an effect on the mood and energy level of the choir while they are in the space rehearsing. Plan for bright, open spaces with bright lighting, but not bright enough to cause a glare. Most lighting companies can tell if the lighting is adequate by conducting tests on the room with light gauges.

10. Does the room have a high ceiling?

Ceilings should be high enough so that the room does not seem smaller than it really is. William Reynolds, in *Building an Effective Music Ministry,* recommends twelve feet, a luxury for most.

11. Does the room have good ventilation?

A room with poor ventilation and air circulation will cause low energy levels and bad moods in the choir during rehearsal.

12. Is the room neat, clean, and pleasing to the eye?

It is amazing what a coat of paint will do for a room. Take a weekend and clean up the choir space. Letting the choir fix up their rehearsal space will give them a sense of ownership and responsibility in caring for it. You will be surprised what a positive effect this will have on your choir.

Many of these criteria may seem completely out of reach; however, if you educate the people in leadership positions in the church about the necessity of having the correct physical conditions in order for the music ministry to grow, the needs could be met more easily than originally thought. If the current situation requires the use of a classroom during the week, and the classroom does not meet these needs, look throughout the entire building to see if there is a better space in which to work. Attitude is everything when it comes to planning for growth. Show a positive attitude on the outside by making the rehearsal areas representative of the pride the choir feels in owning the program.

Chapter Five

The Ever-Important First Rehearsal

E verything has been studied and prepared, the rehearsal space has been spruced up, and several new members are expected at the first rehearsal. The job is complete, right? WRONG!

The job is just beginning. This first rehearsal carries a lot of weight. In order to make the new members feel welcome, plan ahead so that anything that would cause a feeling of alienation is eliminated.

First, be sure that you have enough robes for everyone, including the new members. If robes are not assigned to them, this tells them that there was a lack of preparation, which sends a negative signal. If there are not enough robes, that's all right, but be sure to let the people in the congregation know. Simply announce, "Because the choir has grown so much from the new member campaign, there are not enough robes for everyone. Therefore, we will not wear robes on Sunday." Share this tidbit with the senior pastor so he can announce it from the pulpit. This could yield some contributions for buying additional robes, or better yet, ordering new ones.

Be sure that there is a folder (with pencil) ready to be assigned. This is probably more important than the robe issue. Also be sure to have enough music for everyone. Anticipate how many people will be coming and order extra music, overnight shipping if necessary. The confidence your new members will gain will be worth the additional shipping charges. Never duplicate music. Besides, it is against the law! If you give new members copied music, it tells them that you were unprepared. Besides, they do not want to pay for your bail to get out of jail!

When planning for the first rehearsal, be sure to have name tags for everyone. This will help the new members learn names and faces. Also, have a member of the committee act as chairperson for a reception for the new members. Plan to hold this reception prior to the first rehearsal. This will break the ice, especially if any of the new members were reluctant to come in the first place.

Assign each new member to a "singing buddy" in the choir. This "buddy" will help guide the new member through the pattern of a regular rehearsal and be there to answer any questions. The buddy should be a person from the same voice section.

When planning the musical elements for the first rehearsal, be sure to plan on the light side. You don't want to scare off anyone who's new! Allow time for a long warm-up period. Unison anthems are always good to build confidence in the new members.

If the choir traditionally processes every Sunday, be sure to spend time in the sanctuary during the first rehearsal practicing this. No matter how good the choir is, logistics are usually the most difficult element to master. Leave nothing to chance at the first rehearsal prior to the first Sunday. Go over everything!

Sometime during the week after the first rehearsal, mail a personal letter to new members of the choir telling them how excited you are that they have chosen to become involved. Positive reinforcement will be appreciated. Mail a different letter to your continuing choir members, praising them for their work in preparing for the evening.

Now that the group has grown significantly, communication is more important than before. As soon as possible, send the entire choir a letter complete with the schedule through Christmas and the New Year. Get this information out as soon as possible so people can plan accordingly.

O. K., Someone has my robe again!

Chapter Six

Organization and Communication

Within the Choir

T he larger a group grows, the more important organization and communication are within the group. It is important that internal organizational structure and communication be examined and developed in order to enhance the overall function of the choir.

Officers

Follow parliamentary procedure for electing officers to the choir. Choir officers should, at the least, include a president or chairperson, a treasurer, a sunshine chairperson, and section leaders. A president or chairperson will be in charge of organizing any special events outside of the choir's regular responsibilities, such as dinners or a new choir robe committee.

The treasurer will handle the choir's money. The choir will need some money for special get-togethers throughout the year, buying supplies for the sunshine chairperson, and other monetary necessities.

The sunshine chairperson handles the personal details that make a small group more successful and meaningful. This person is usually in charge of mailing cards for birthdays, anniversaries, sympathy, and so on.

Section leaders are responsible for the smooth operation of the section. Each section leader should have the names and phone numbers of everyone in his or her section. The section leaders are usually the first link in the phone chain (to be discussed later in this chapter).

Policies and Procedures Manual

A policies and procedures manual will help keep communication open within the group. It will also be an asset to the new members of the choir who need to learn the "ins and outs" of what to do and when—things the present choir members probably know. Some basic items to include in the manual are:

1. Rehearsal times
2. Signing out for missed Sundays and rehearsals (helps you plan accordingly)
3. Basic outline of rehearsal format
4. Sunday morning procedures to prepare for worship
5. Procedures during worship
   a. Introit
   b. Singing hymns (when to sing unison or in parts)
   c. Processional and recessional
   d. How to stand in the loft (folders always open, or closed when not singing)
   e. Special Communion Sunday instructions
6. Procedures after worship
   a. Turning in music
   b. Proper care for robes

Other general things to include could be:

1. Perfume and jewelry policies
2. Robe cleaning instructions
3. Guidelines that aid the sunshine chairperson in determining when to send cards and letters
4. Guidelines for rehearsals when the weather is inclement

The best way to approach preparing a policy manual is to enlist the aid of the choir officers. If the governing body of the choir is used in helping establish guidelines, the pressure is removed from the director and gives ownership of the program to the group. It is important to have all of these details in writing. It will save the director from certain problems later. Be sure to use your imagination in order to cover every aspect possible.

Choir Phone Chain and Directory

Set up a phone chain within the choir. There will be times when everyone in the choir needs to be informed quickly. Examples are a change in the rehearsal schedule because of bad weather, the death of a choir member, the death of a family member of someone in the choir. Be ready when something happens. The normal procedure for starting the phone chain is for the director to call the section leaders. The section leaders then call three or four people in the section, who in turn, call the remainder of the section. Organizing this phone chain sends a signal, a signal that you care about the choir and want to keep them informed.

Place this phone chain in a directory along with personal information about everyone in the choir, including addresses, phone numbers, places of employment, birthday and anniversary information, and the section in which they sing. Make this booklet available to everyone in the choir as soon as possible.

Developing a Choir Newsletter

Members of the choir need to be kept current on the events involving the choir. A newsletter is an easy way to do this. The newsletter should be neat, clean, and professional looking. Items to include in the newsletter are:

1. Choir members' birthdays and anniversaries for the current month
2. The rehearsal order for the evening, complete with dates each anthem is scheduled, and highlighting the anthem for the coming week
3. Any other special instructions for the upcoming Sunday
4. Any announcements related to the choir schedule
5. Calendar of events to the end of the season, that is, from September to the New Year, and from the New Year to Easter, and from Easter to the end of the choir season
6. Any other information that will aid in the smooth operation of the group

Be sure to keep the newsletter readable. Keep announcements short and to the point. Simply list facts when possible. Place this newsletter at the entrance to the rehearsal area where people check their attendance. After rehearsal, mail the newsletter to those not in rehearsal. Doing so sends the signal that these persons were missed. Also, the newsletter informs those absent of what was done in rehearsal, what the anthem is for the upcoming Sunday, and any new announcements and schedule changes. In order to save time, keep a supply of current mailing labels available to use for the newsletter and other scheduled choir mailings. The simplest way to get started is to use a standard sheet of 8½-by-11-inch paper, divided into sections with a heading for each section. Arrange the page so that when the 8½-by-11-inch page is folded in half horizontally, the return address is on the outside in the upper left-hand corner. Staple or tape it closed, place a label on it to the member of the choir not present, stamp it with postage, and mail it. In usual cases, the person should receive the letter before the upcoming Sunday.

Newsletter Name

Date   Rehearsal time

....

Birthdays and Anniversaries
Rehearsal Order
Announcements
Calendar of Events

Within the Congregation

Developing a Program Guide for the Season

In the late summer, formulate a document that will lay out the entire music ministry offerings for the coming season. In many churches, there already are established traditions, especially during seasons like Advent and Christmas, Easter and Pentecost. Use these special programs to begin developing a schedule for the coming season. The pamphlet should include the names and rehearsal times of all of the choirs (including handbell groups), special performances and musical program dates throughout the year (including dates the children's choirs sing), information about the people who will be staffing the music ministry, goals and dreams for the future of the program, and a music ministry registration form. The registration form will help you to know how many to expect at the first rehearsals for all of the choirs.

It is also good to develop a faith statement for the music ministry explaining the ideals the ministry will strive to uphold. The faith statement needs to be rooted in the Scriptures and represent the function of the music ministry in the church. By mailing this booklet to everyone in the congregation, you are educating them about what the music ministry has to offer, the responsibilities of the participants as well as the director, and why it is important to the spiritual life of the church. In most churches, the congregation sees the music director or organist once a week on Sunday. This booklet will let the entire congregation know what is going on, what the job requirements are, and what the goals are for the year. Compiling the information for the book will take some advance planning, but doing this sends a message that the director is organized and that the music ministry is important to the life of the church.

Use of Church Mailings

Use the regular church mailings to remind people of upcoming events. For example, if there is a special Christmas program coming up next month, ask for the front of the church newsletter to highlight this special event.

Send a Special Invitation

To add a touch of class, have a professional printer create invitations to special events and mail them to the entire congregation.

Keep the invitation postcard size since it is cheaper to mail a postcard than a letter. When possible, conserve resources by including this invitation with another bulk mailing going out at the same time, such as pledge statements or seasonal offering envelopes. If the invitation is printed on a postcard, save time and money by preprinting the return address and bulk rate stamp on the other side. This way, the only thing you need to do is to add the mailing labels. Members of the church feel special when they receive an invitation to a music event. It also serves as a reminder, which helps increase attendance at the event.

The Music Ministry of
(YOUR CHURCH NAME)
cordially invites you to attend

A Candlelight Service of Lessons and Carols
Sunday, December 21, 1994
7:00 P.M.
(Prelude begins at 6:30 P.M.)

Music to be presented by. . . .

Chapter Seven

Special Events

T he weekly routine of coming to rehearsal and singing on Sunday morning can become tedious. Spice up the regular routine with special events.

Birthday Parties

At the beginning or end of each month, plan a social time to celebrate the birthdays and anniversaries of the month. It could be planned either before or after the rehearsal. Keep it on the same night as choir rehearsal so people do not have to come out for another evening event.

Seasonal Get-Togethers

Plan a get-together in the fall when the season is just starting. This informal, social time will help everybody learn names and faces. Plan a cook-out, swimming party, or covered-dish dinner *away* from the church if possible (this will depend on the size of the choir). Taking the event away from the church will enable people to relax and be more comfortable. Plan another party just before Christmas and include a tacky, "white elephant" gift exchange. In the spring, have another get-together before the season is over.

Planning social time above and beyond the regular rehearsal will give the group a more personable atmosphere.

Choir Retreats

One event planned for the fall could be a weekend retreat. A retreat can act as a time of spiritual renewal, skill development, and rejuvenation. Take the choir on a retreat *away* from the church or the town in which you live. If you plan a retreat close to your town, it will be too convenient for choir members to come and go and miss the opportunity for fellowship and development. Go to your conference retreat center or other appropriate place. Be sure that the facilities have necessary rehearsal facilities.

A good use of time and a boost for skill development would be a weekend retreat with an outside clinician. Directors always strive for good elements of singing like breath support, tone, and vowel blending. When these elements are stressed by another person, the choir members see them in a new light. I have seen choirs transformed over a weekend retreat. One word of caution: Be sure that the guest clinician teaches the same principles of vocal production as those of the director.

If possible, include a special event in the weekend, like a campfire, special dedication worship service on Sunday morning, or singing at a local church. This is also an excellent opportunity to spend extended time rehearsing larger works planned for the upcoming year. Christmas music is always a good draw for people to attend the retreat. Plan the retreat well enough in advance so people can adjust their schedules accordingly. Good times for a retreat are early fall and right after Christmas.

Be sure to plan relaxation and fellowship time into the weekend schedule.

Trips

Trips always add special excitement for the choir, *so,* when possible, plan a trip. A trip can be missional or pleasurable in nature. Consider a wide range of possibilities from interesting geographical destinations to special workshops and conferences.

An easy way to get started is to plan several smaller trips initially. Ask your choir members for possible contacts in certain areas of the country and use these contacts to plan a trip itinerary. Also, look in the area in which you live to see if it would be possible to sing at a larger church. For example, if your church is located near the East Coast, consider Washington, D.C.; it is always a good place to sing, and there are enough things to do that you could make it a weekend trip. Here again, use your imagination to create possibilities.

If you are really adventuresome, plan a trip overseas to England, Spain, Austria, or other places in Europe. Developing a mission statement for the trip will help when presenting the trip to the choir and the congregation. Look into the history of the church and develop a trip around that history. If you belong to a Presbyterian church, plan a choir trip to study the birth of the Presbyterian church. If you are Methodist, plan a trip to England to study Methodist history.

Advance planning is crucial in preparing for a trip. It is not uncommon to plan a trip up to two years in advance.

Fund Raising for Trips

Fund raising for trips, or for anything in general, can be time-consuming. In order to make as much profit as possible, be creative in developing ideas for money raising. Plan on doing things that yield a high dollar amount. Bake sales and car washes are great, but how many would have to be done to

raise $10,000! Here are a few large-scale money-making sug-
gestions.

    1. Make a choir recording. If researched and handled care-
fully, a choir recording can yield up to 80 percent profit.
Select a season of the year to feature on the recording,
like Christmas. Record the music in the late spring or
early summer, or even right after Christmas, produce the
recording over the summer, and have it ready for sale by
the following fall.

    2. Auction a car. If the church has a member who is an
automobile dealer, see if he or she will donate a car to
the church to auction off by silent auction to the general
public. Proceeds would be 100 percent.

    3. Dinners. Dinners are always good because food can be
marked up a great deal in order to make profit. Have a
"Tasters Tea" by invitation only, or have a "Fish Bake"
every Friday during Lent. Since the church is a nonprofit
organization, many people will donate food items to be
prepared. If all or most of the food is donated, profits
are in the 80 to 100 percent range.

Before undertaking any fund-raiser, clear the idea with the
finance committee in your church. If things were planned
properly, a music ministry person on the finance committee
can promote the fund-raiser to the committee for approval.
Also, think of fund-raisers that can be done outside the
church. It will be difficult to meet your goals when you are
always asking the same people for money.

*O. K. choir plebes, the first and hardest drill for
any choir member to master is the processional!*

Chapter Eight

Special Projects

T his chapter will discuss several different projects the
choir can take on to help them create a sense of
belonging and pride in what they are giving to the
church.

Bell Banners

Bell banners are a beautiful way for the choir to express
their appreciation for the musical training they have experi-
enced. Have each member of the choir donate a bell in honor
or in memory of someone who was influential in their musical
training. When all of the bells are turned in, complete with the
name of the person to whom each is dedicated, place the list of
dedications on the wall in the choir room. Be sure to stress
that the bells are regular bells about one to two inches in
height. Try to stay away from jingle bells unless you plan to
only use the banner at Christmas! Most fabric and craft stores
have small, brass bells in stock that are perfect to place on the
banner. Use your imagination in constructing a frame for the
banner. One simple way is to purchase PVC pipe and make a
T using the appropriate connectors and end pieces. Spray
paint the pipe an appropriate color, hang multicolored ribbons
from the cross bar, and attach the bells to the ribbons at vari-
ous heights. When the banner is used in a processional, the

loose ribbons flow back while the ribbons with the bells hang down and ring, creating a beautiful effect. Every time the banner is used, it reminds the choristers of their musical heritage. To further help, there are many books available on the design and construction of liturgical banners.

History of the Music Ministry

Another way to create a sense of pride and ownership is to create a booklet telling the history of the music ministry of the church. For some churches, this book could be quite lengthy. For other ministries just getting started, the information would be easier to compile.

The church should have a way of documenting its history. If bulletins and newsletters are regularly stored as records, researching these items will be easy. Another avenue to take is interviewing some of the oldest members of the church, inquiring about their favorite memories of the music ministry in years past. On the wall in the choir room, place a chart documenting the historical order of music directors and organists (this information can be found in old bulletins and newsletters). Studying the history of the church, and specifically, the music ministry, will create a sense of ownership and appreciation and even help determine a future course for the ministry.

Honorary Plaques

Choir directors all over the country are amazed at the people who have served in their choirs for years and years. In the choir room, create a "Hall of Fame" or "Wall of Dedication" to honor those who have given years of service to the choir. Two landmark years to honor are twenty-five years of service and fifty years of service. Anybody who has sung in the same church choir for more than fifty years should receive a medal!

The least we can do as directors is recognize these people and use them as examples for others to follow, especially today's young people.

Choir Dedication Sunday

Pick a Sunday sometime during the year and proclaim it "Choir Dedication Sunday." Create a special service for recognizing and commissioning the choirs of the church. A good time to do a commissioning service is in the fall. The spring is a good time to have a Choir Recognition Sunday.

Dedication to the music ministry goes beyond dedication to almost any other ministry in the church. When you think about it, the musicians of the church meet at least four times as often as any other group in the church with four times the workload. The choir's main function is to provide functional music for the worship service in order to glorify God. This should be enough of a reason to sing in the choir. However, in today's secular world, people need to be reaffirmed in what they are doing. Most churches have a commissioning service for the people newly elected to serve on the church's committees. A dedication or commissioning Sunday for the music ministry is a great way to affirm everyone involved.

Chapter Nine

Music Leadership in the Community

Musicians today are faced with several serious problems. Fewer and fewer people are going into the music profession, especially the profession of church music. This shortage of musicians is having a profound impact on the musical life of the church. Many churches cannot find a qualified person even to play the organ on Sunday; therefore, some have turned to electronic keyboards out of necessity.

This change is both good and bad for the church. Today's younger generation generally likes to hear in church the kind of music they hear on popular radio stations, and an electronic keyboard can certainly aid in creating this musical style. But one has to ask, Where is the heritage? When popular music changes, will these churches change their musical style again? In these situations, is the church assuming a leadership role or a passive role by changing to suit demands from society? Think about it. If today's baby boomers want more of a popular sound in church, then what does the church do when today's youth come of age? It is intriguing that as this book is being written, one of the most popular recordings is of a Gregorian chant from a monastic community in Spain! Maybe what people are really looking for is the focus and stability tradition can give.

The best way to meet the needs of every generation is to create a music ministry that encompasses *all musical styles,* including contemporary Christian and Gregorian chant. By creating a ministry that is all-encompassing, you've created something to which every person at every age can relate. This, in turn, broadens the potential list of new members.

Another worrisome problem is the shrinking church music budget. People are reluctant to pledge to the church, given today's uncertain financial picture. People, on the average, are pledging less to the church, while non-pledge, plate collections are increasing dramatically. This signifies that people will give gladly when they can but will not commit to a certain amount. The uncertainty makes it difficult for church finance committees to produce a budget.

This problem calls on the church musician to be resourceful when planning and budgeting. If the music budget is shrinking, fund-raisers may be in order. If money is donated to the memorial committee, use this money to purchase new music and place a "memorial plate" on each octavo stating that the anthem was purchased with memorial moneys given in memory of a certain individual. Also, try to find some patrons in the church who would be willing to help finance guest instrumentalists for special events. Another source of money is the American Federation of Musicians. The federation has a trust fund that helps pay union musicians the church would use for special services. Be advised that the union will not pay for musicians used in a regular worship service but will provide moneys for special concerts. Be resourceful in creating additional moneys for the music budget.

Another problem that is just surfacing is the threat to music programs in the public schools! Schools are also victims of the budget ax, and the children of baby boomers are growing quickly, leaving a glut of teachers in the classroom. Most state governments appropriate so much money per student.

The government mandates certain guidelines for public education but provides no additional funding for these mandates. Enrollment is declining simply because there are fewer students and schools are faced with major budget cuts. Unfortunately, the first thing to go, after laying off teachers, is usually the music class, not extracurricular activities like sports. When looking at public education throughout the country, the first music classes to go are the elementary music classes, then the junior high classes.

Today's educators seem shortsighted. Do they not realize that by cutting music education for that early age, they are removing the very soul from the children's education? What is more uplifting than children's voices raised in song! Do they not realize that today's elementary children are tomorrow's junior high and high school students, and if these children don't receive any musical experience in the early years, they will not be involved in the high school years? Where will that leave the good high school programs surviving today? Before long, music will become extinct at every age level in schools!

We can hope this trend will stop, and soon. The reason this issue is so critical is that what happens in public music education has a dramatic impact on the church's music program. On the average, most choirs hold rehearsals for groups once a week. If music programs are in place in schools, music education can take place every day. When this daily education is lost, the church music program suffers as well.

In this dim light, a flame of possibility burns brighter than ever for the church. What a wonderful opportunity for churches to pick up where public education is failing. If you want your church and the music program to grow, create a top-notch children's music program. (Better yet, use the recently published children's choir curriculum, *Church Music for Children*, available from Abingdon Press. This multi-component program has everything you need right out of the box and is designed for use by professionals and volunteers alike. —*Editor*) An added bonus is that if you can get the kids, you will get the parents! Look in the community and try to find a musical area that needs to be addressed and then address the need. If elementary music is being cut from the schools, the church should create programs to meet the needs of these children. It will take a lot of work and a lot of planning, but the benefits are worth it.

Chapter Ten

In Conclusion

The key to a vibrant, growing music ministry is diversity. Selected musical offerings should meet the needs of a child as well as a senior citizen. By creating a program that meets the needs of this wide age range, you are creating a drawing card for all people. People will be attracted to a good, diverse, high-quality program. If this kind of program is developed, the people will come. It takes time to develop a program, as well as good interpersonal skills on the part of the director, but once the public knows what is being offered and who is in charge of it, they will be attracted to the program. This attraction, when coupled with all of the ideas presented in this book, can lead to unprecedented growth in the music ministry. The most important element to keep in mind is to do everything to the glory of God Almighty. Without this one element, we will surely fail.

It is a calling to work in church music ministry—a calling that should not be taken lightly. The Scriptures state that everything that is done for the glory of God needs to be done as well as possible. The church is not a place for poor workmanship and half-hearted dedication. It will be hard, sometimes overwhelming work, but with the right support, resources, and guidance, a lay volunteer in church music can create a successful music ministry.

.5171

90728

LINCOLN CHRISTIAN COLLEGE AND SEMINARY

782.5171 D677
Donathan, David F.
How does your choir grow?

DEMCO

3 4711 00086 1544